What colour?

Lucy und Fred sind bei ihrer Oma zu Besuch. Sie wohnt in einem großen, alten Haus, in dem es viel zu entdecken gibt. Sie gehen auf den Dachboden und finden eine große Kiste, **a big box.** Hier kannst du sehen, was sie alles finden.

Suche alle Gegenstände oben im Bild und male sie in den richtigen Farben an.

The spider is black.
The knife is grey and black.
The flag of Germany is black, red and yellow.
The teddy is brown.
The shoes are blue.
The bats are black.
The socks are green.
The gold is gold.
The skis are pink.
The book is red.

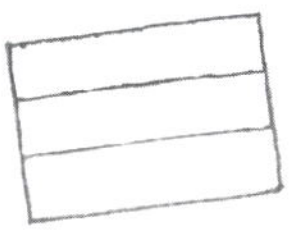

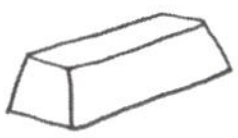

Lösung

Hello! My name is ...

Stell dich vor!

My name is: ____________________

My birthday is: ____________________

I live in: ____________________

My favourite colour is: ____________________

I like: ____________________

I don't like: ____________________

Lösung

Du kannst so einen Steckbrief auf Englisch von dir schreiben. Zeige ihn deinen Eltern und Freunden.

This is me

Male hier ein Bild von dir selbst hin oder klebe ein Foto ein.

Schreibe jetzt drei Sätze auf Englisch auf, die dich beschreiben. Benutze dabei die Wörter in den folgenden Listen. Nehme für jeden Satz ein Wort aus jeder Zeile. So könnte zum Beispiel dein erster Satz lauten:

My hair is long. – Meine Haare sind lang.

My	eyes	are	long
	hair	is	short
	mouth		blue
	teeth		brown
			blond
			green
			red
			black
			white

1. ______________________________

2. ______________________________

3. ______________________________

Lösung

Wie siehst du aus?

Wörter, die du nicht kennst, schlägst du im Wörterbuch nach. Schwierige Wörter kannst du noch einmal aufschreiben.

The family

a. Verbinde jeweils das richtige englische Wort mit dem deutschen Wort.

mum	Schwester
brother	Oma
grandma	Mama
dad	Bruder
granddad	Opa
sister	Papa

b. This is Lucy's family. Das ist Lucys Familie. Trage die Namen der Familienmitglieder in die Kästchen.

Lösung

a. mum – Mama, brother – Bruder, grandma – Oma, dad – Papa, grandad – Opa, sister – Schwester

b. im Uhrzeigersinn von oben links:
dad, mum, sister, brother

Who is this?

Wer hat sich hier versteckt? Nimm einen Bleistift und verbinde der Reihe nach die Punkte, um es herauszufinden. Trage die englischen Begriffe in die Kästchen ein.

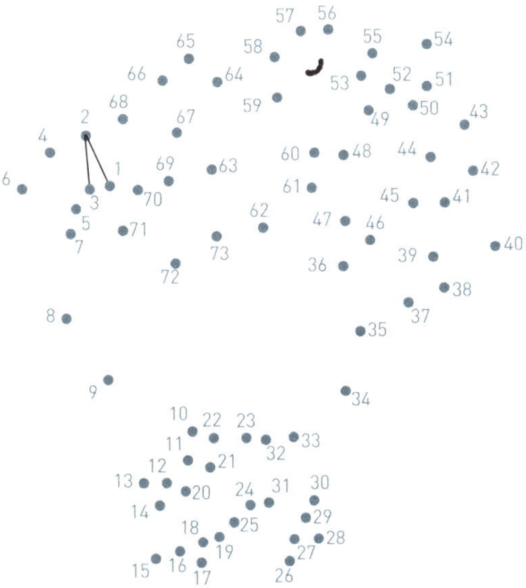

1. | | | | |

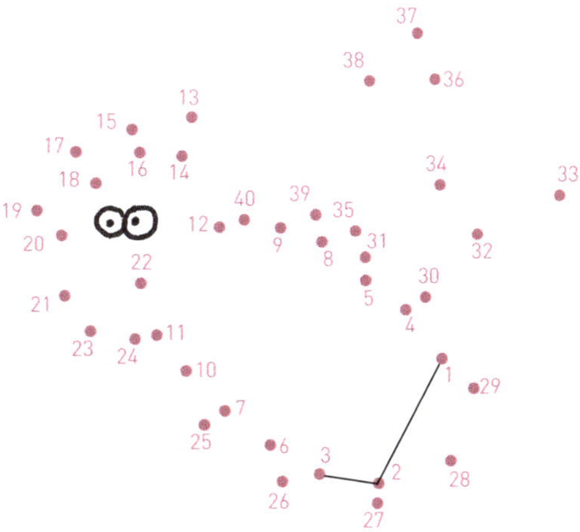

2. | | | |

Lösung

1 = duck, **2** = pig

Holidays

Ordne diese besonderen Tag in der Reihenfolge, in der sie im Jahr stattfinden. Wenn du weißt, wann sie genau stattfinden, kannst du das Datum dazuschreiben.

Easter

Valentine's Day

Christmas

Halloween

New Year's Eve

1. ____________________
2. ____________________
3. ____________________
4. ____________________
5. ____________________

Lösung

1. Valentine's Day (14th February)
2. Easter (March or April)
3. Halloween (31st October)
4. Christmas (25th December)
5. New Year's Eve (31st December)

Food and drink

Verbinde die englischen Wörter jeweils mit dem richtigen Bild.

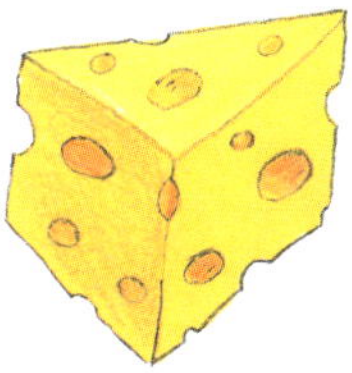
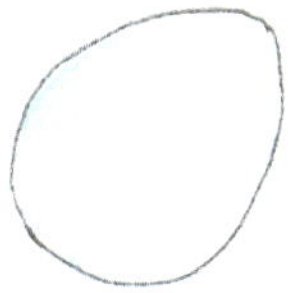

milk

muffin

bread

banana

coffee

egg

cheese

apples

muesli

water

orange juice

ham

Lösung

milk
muffin
bread
banana
coffee
egg
cheese
apples
muesli
water
orange juice
ham

At the table

Zum Essen und Trinken braucht man Geschirr und Besteck.
Ergänze die Sätze mit den richtigen Utensilien.

1. I eat muesli with a ____spoon____.

2. I drink hot chocolate in a ________________.

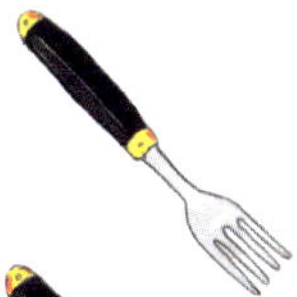

3. I eat spaghetti with a ________________.

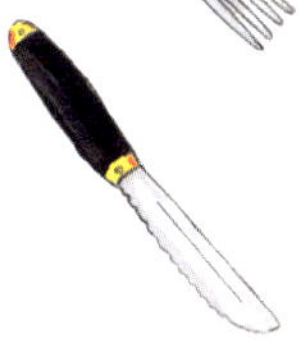

4. I cut bread with a ________________.

5. I drink water in a ________________.

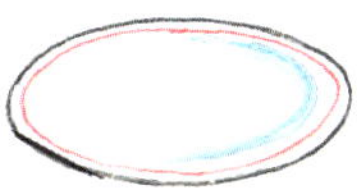

6. I eat a sandwich on a ________________.

Lösung

1. spoon
2. cup
3. fork
4. knife
5. glass
6. plate

Find the words

Kreuze an, welche Wörter du schon auf Englisch sagen kannst.

Nun schau, ob du die acht Wörter im Raster findest.
Die Wörter sind alle vorwärts zu lesen – entweder waagerecht →, senkrecht ↓ oder diagonal ↘. Male einen Kringel um jedes Wort, das du findest.

A	C	V	I	N	H	C	X	B	E
K	B	A	N	A	N	A	Y	M	L
W	R	J	L	S	I	R	M	Z	C
G	E	H	F	A	B	Q	K	T	H
N	A	F	A	P	P	L	E	O	E
U	D	R	Z	F	D	D	T	Q	E
M	O	X	M	U	F	F	I	N	S
O	I	L	T	X	R	Y	W	A	E
W	W	L	S	Q	J	H	O	G	C
J	Q	O	K	F	W	A	T	E	R

Lösung

A	C	V	I	N	H	C	X	B	E
K	B	A	N	A	N	A	Y	M	L
W	R	J	L	S	I	R	M	Z	C
G	E	H	F	A	B	Q	K	T	H
N	A	F	A	P	P	L	E	O	E
U	D	R	Z	F	D	D	T	Q	E
M	O	X	M	U	F	F	I	N	S
O	I	L	T	X	R	Y	W	A	E
W	W	L	S	Q	J	H	O	G	C
J	Q	O	K	F	W	A	T	E	R

In the bedroom

Was stimmt? Schau dir das Bild genau an und kreuze an, was richtig ist.

1. There is a cupboard.	☐ yes	☐ no
2. There is one bed.	☐ yes	☐ no
3. There is a clock.	☐ yes	☐ no
4. The beds are red.	☐ yes	☐ no
5. There are five books on the shelf.	☐ yes	☐ no
6. There is a lamp.	☐ yes	☐ no
7. There is a computer.	☐ yes	☐ no

cupboard – der Schrank
shelf – das Regal

Lösung

1. yes, **2.** no, **3.** yes, **4.** yes, **5.** no, **6.** yes, **7.** no

Lucy's house

Lucy beschreibt Fred ihr Haus. Male ein Bild davon.

Lösung

Das **Haus** hat eine blaue Tür, grüne Fenster, ein rotes Dach und einen Kamin. Es hat fünf Fenster und einen Garten mit Bäumen und Blumen.

The right clothes

Es ist Dezember und draußen ist es sehr kalt, **very cold**. Lucy und Fred wollen in den Weihnachtsferien verreisen, können sich aber nicht einigen, wohin. Fred möchte gerne Ski fahren aber Lucy möchte lieber dorthin, wo es auch im Winter warm und sonnig, **warm and sunny,** ist. Wer packt was in seinen eigenen Koffer? Schreibe die richtigen Wörter in die Koffer.

Lösung

Lucy nimmt mit: sandals, swimsuit, shorts, sunglasses, T-Shirt, sun hat

Fred nimmt mit: pullover, trousers, coat, scarf, gloves, boots

Where are they?

In dem Raster sind die englischen Wörter für die folgenden Körperteile versteckt. Findest du sie? Die Wörter sind alle vorwärts zu lesen – entweder waagerecht →, senkrecht ↓ oder diagonal ↘.

Kopf Po Hand Mund Bein Arm Finger Augen Hals Bauch

W	H	X	C	V	M	R	L	A	B
E	A	I	Y	L	O	E	Q	E	J
R	N	R	P	F	U	U	B	J	G
T	D	T	M	V	T	Z	O	I	F
U	F	S	E	U	H	O	T	M	H
M	G	E	P	F	C	V	T	S	D
M	K	H	E	A	D	M	O	A	N
Y	E	J	S	I	B	Y	M	X	E
A	S	H	E	Y	E	S	R	W	C
F	I	N	G	E	R	K	S	A	K

Lösung

W	H	X	C	V	M	R	L	A	B
E	A	I	Y	L	O	E	Q	E	J
R	N	R	P	F	U	U	B	J	G
T	D	T	M	V	T	Z	O	I	F
U	F	S	E	U	H	O	T	M	H
M	G	E	P	F	C	V	T	S	D
M	K	H	E	A	D	M	O	A	N
Y	E	J	S	I	B	Y	M	X	E
A	S	H	E	Y	E	S	R	W	C
F	I	N	G	E	R	K	S	A	K

Where?

Schau dir die Bilder an und vervollständige anschließend die Sätze. Ergänze jeweils die richtige Präposition, das heißt das richtige Verhältniswort.

1. Fips is ________ the bed.
2. Lucy is ________ the bed.

3. The books are ________ the shelf.
4. The clock is ________ the shelf.

5. Lucy is sitting ________ the armchair.
6. The armchair is ________ the window.

7. The picture is ________ the suitcase.
8. The chair is ________ the suitcase.

Tipp: Die Wörter, die Fips dir zeigt, helfen dir, die Sätze zu verstehen.

Lösung

1. in
2. next to
3. on
4. under
5. in
6. in front of
7. behind
8. next to

Fruit and vegetables

Kreuze an, welche Wörter du bereits auf Englisch kennst und schreibe die Namen der **fruit and vegetables**, des Obst und Gemüses, auf die Linien.

1. ______________

2. ______________

3. ______________

4. ______________

5. ______________

6. ______________

7. ______________

8. ______________

9. ______________

10. ______________

11. ______________

12. ______________

Lösung

1. Banane – banana
2. Kirsche – cherry
3. Apfel – apple
4. Kürbis – pumpkin
5. Orange – orange
6. Gurke – cucumber
7. Birne – pear
8. Zitrone – lemon
9. Tomate – tomato
10. Blaubeeren – blueberries
11. Karotte – carrot
12. Erdbeere – strawberry

My house

Wie sieht es bei dir zu Hause aus? Zähle die Möbelstücke und beantworte die Fragen. Zähle auf Englisch!

1. How many beds are there?

   z. B. In my house there are four beds.

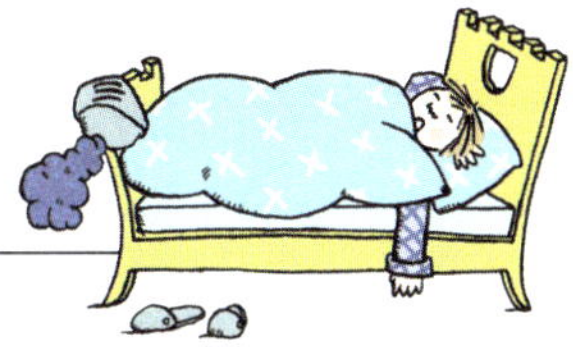

2. How many tables are there?

3. How many sofas are there?

4. How many chairs are there?

5. How many showers are there?

6. How many lamps are there?

7. How many pictures are there?

8. How many shelves are there?

Lösung

Wenn du ein Wort nicht kennst, schlage es im Wörterbuch nach. Du kannst es hier auch noch einmal aufschreiben.

Which house?

Welche Beschreibung passt zu welchem Haus? Verbinde.

1. ☐
This house has a garden.
It has two windows.

2. ☐
This house is very small.
It has a green door.

A

B

C

D

3. ☐
This house is very big.
It has lots of windows.
The Queen of England
lives in this house.

4. ☐
This house is very tall.
It has four windows and
a green door.

Lösung

1. D, **2.** A, **3.** B, **4.** C

What's the weather like?

Kannst du jedem Satz das passende Bild zuordnen?

1. The sun is shining. ◯

2. It's raining. ◯

3. It's foggy. ◯

4. It's snowing. ◯

5. It's windy. ◯

6. There's a storm. ◯

What's the weather like? Und wie ist das Wetter bei dir heute? Schreibe hier auf Englisch hin, wie das Wetter ist.

Lösung

1. D, **2.** A, **3.** F, **4.** B, **5.** E, **6.** C

Around the year

Im Herbst gehen Lucy und Fips gerne spazieren und sammeln bunte Blätter oder lassen ihren Drachen, **their kite**, steigen. Sie überlegen, was sie am nächsten Tag machen werden und malen davon ein Bild. Wenn du die Flächen so anmalst, wie angegeben, wirst du sehen, was sie vorhaben!

1 **red**	3 **green**	5 **orange**	7 **black**	9 **pink**
2 **blue**	4 **yellow**	6 **brown**	8 **white**	10 **purple**

Lösung

Colours

Hier kannst du die Farben auf Englisch üben. Verbinde jeweils die Wörter mit dem richtigen Pinsel, so wie im Beispiel.

- donkey
- pumpkin
- pig
- black sheep
- tomato
- white sheep
- frog
- chick

Lösung

donkey – grey

pumpkin – orange

pig – pink

black sheep – black

tomato – red

white sheep – white

frog – green

chick – yellow

School words

In dem Bleistift sind die Namen von fünf Gegenständen versteckt.
Male einen Kringel um jedes Wort herum.

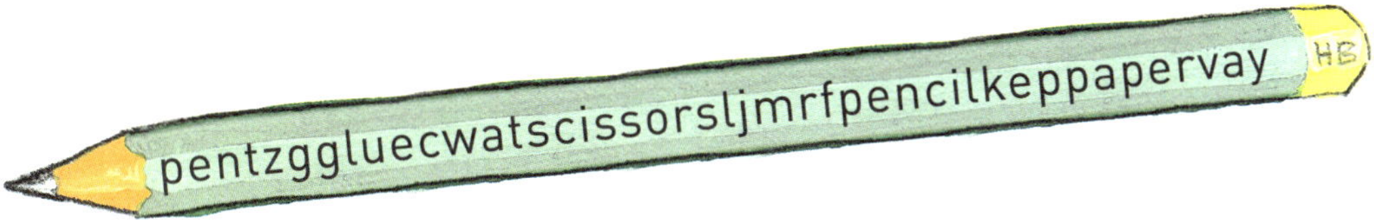

My schoolbag

Schreibe hier fünf Gegenstände auf, die sich in deinem Schulranzen, **in your schoolbag**, befinden.

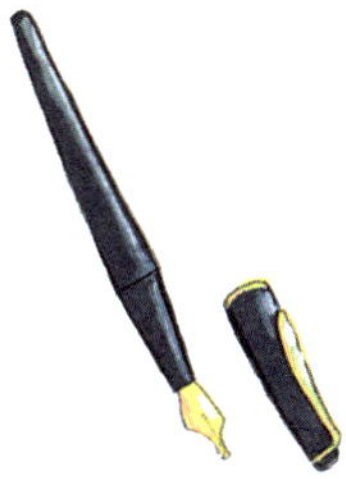

____

____

____

____

____

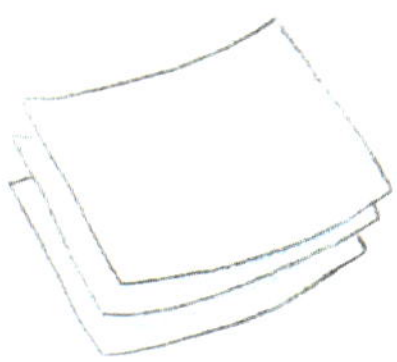

Lösung

pen tzg **glue** cwat **scissors** ljmrf **pencil** kep **paper** vay

pen Füller

glue Klebstoff

scissors Schere

pencil Stift

paper Papier

Missing

a. Oops, wer hat hier Buchstaben geklaut? In jedem Wort fehlt ein Buchstabe. Ergänze die fehlenden Buchstaben, damit die Wörter wieder richtig geschrieben sind.

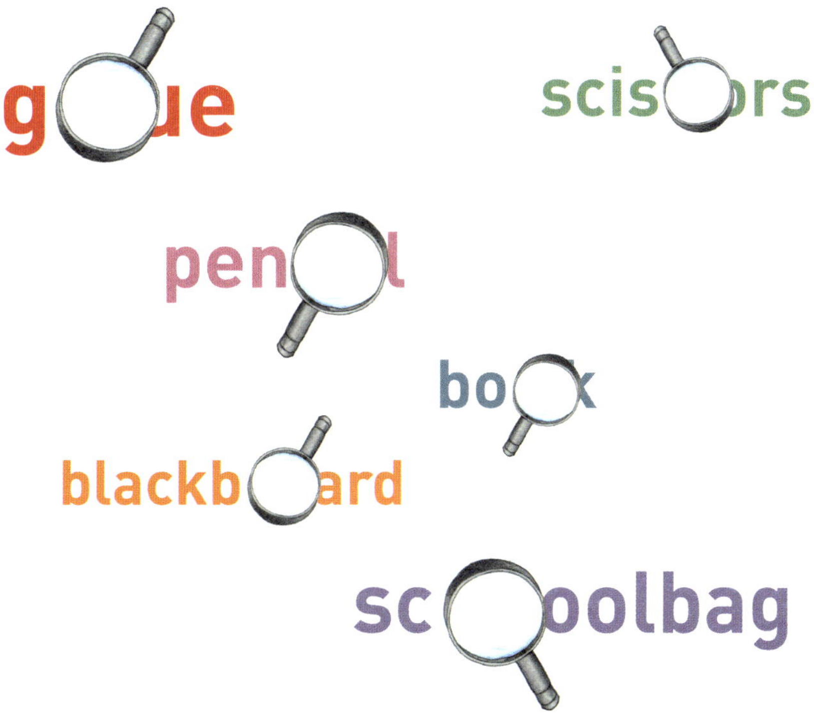

b. Mit den fehlenden Buchstaben kannst du außerdem diesen Satz vervollständigen. Sortiere sie in die richtige Reihenfolge und finde das Lösungswort:

Lucy and Fred are at ________________.

Lösung

a. glue, scissors, pencil, book, blackboard, schoolbag

b. Lucy and Fred are at **school**.

Free time

Fred, Lucy und Fips sind in ihrer Freizeit immer sehr beschäftigt! Verbinde jeden Satz jeweils mit dem passenden Bild.

A

B

1. Lucy is **swimming**.
2. Fred is **cycling**.
3. Lucy is **painting**.
4. Fips is **reading**.
5. Fred is **playing football**.
6. Lucy is **singing**.
7. Fips is **eating**.
8. Fred and Fips are **playing a game**.

C

D

E

F

G

H

Lösung

1. A
2. F
3. H
4. B
5. E
6. G
7. C
8. D

At the beach

Dieses Jahr machen Lucy und ihre Familie Urlaub am Strand.
Welche Wörter haben mit dem Strand zu tun? Kreise sie ein.

bikini

shell

sea

bus

sand boots sandcastle

mountain

sun

lighthouse

beach

shorts

beachball

Easter egg

sunglasses

sandals

bed

seagull

scarf

suncream

picnic

swimming trunks

towel

plane

Lösung

bikini, shell, sea, sand, lighthouse, beach, beachball, seagull, swimming trunks, towel, suncream, sunglasses, sandcastle, sun, shorts, sandals, picnic

Who sits where?

Das sind Schüler der Klasse 3b. Alle Kinder hören aufmerksam zu, während der Lehrer, Mr Black, etwas erklärt. Alle Kinder bis auf eines … Finde heraus, wer sich von Fips ablenken lässt. Lies dir den Text genau durch und schreibe die Namen der Kinder unter die Schreibtische.

Ella sits next to Lucy. Sophie sits behind Ella. Sophie sits between Tom and Maxi. Philipp sits in front of Maxi.

Lucy

Lösung

Tom	Sophie	Maxi
Lucy	Ella	Philipp

Please listen, **Maxi**!

My Bike

Beantworte die folgenden Fragen.

1. I have got a bike. ☐ yes ☐ no

2. My bike is ________________ (z. B. **red**, **blue** ...).

3. This is my bike:

4. I like cycling. ☐ yes ☐ no

5. I go to school on my bike. ☐ yes ☐ no

6. My family has _______ bikes.

Lösung

Wichtige **Fahrradwörter** sind außerdem:

to ride a bike mit dem Fahrrad fahren

bike lane Fahrradweg

mountain bike Mountainbike

racing bike Rennrad

What is it?

a. Kreuze an, welche Wörter du bereits auf Englisch kennst.

1. ____________

2. ____________

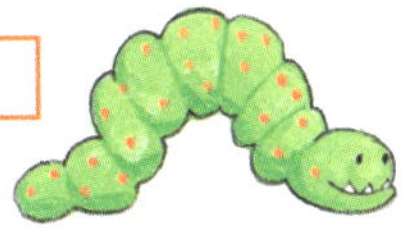

3. ____________

4. ____________

5. ____________

6. ____________

7. ____________

8. ____________

9. ____________

b. Wähle zu jedem Bild jeweils das richtige Wort und schreibe es auf die Linie.

bird **tree** **leaf** **butterfly** **worm**

caterpillar **grass** **flower** **bee**

Lösung

1. tree
2. flower
3. caterpillar
4. leaf
5. bird
6. grass
7. bee
8. worm
9. butterfly

Which animal?

a. Fips riecht etwas Interessantes.
Schreibe die englischen Wörter in die Kästchen.

					1			

		2		

3		

4			

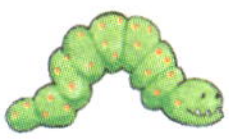

						5				

6			

b. Einige Buchstaben sind nummeriert. Schreibe sie in das Lösungsfeld und du findest heraus, welches Tier Fips entdeckt hat.

1	2	3	4	5	6

c. Auf Deutsch heißt es: ______________________________

Lösung

a. Von oben: butterfly, grass, bee, bird, caterpillar, tree

b. rabbit

c. Kaninchen

One dog – two dogs

Alle Wörter stehen in der Einzahl. Schreibe hier die Mehrzahl auf.

one dog	– two ___________	one elephant	– two ___________
one sheep	– two ___________	one lion	– two ___________
one tiger	– two ___________	one cow	– two ___________
one bear	– two ___________	one pig	– two ___________
one bird	– two ___________	one spider	– two ___________

Who is it?

Welche Tiere werden hier beschrieben?

1. This animal is brown and white. It gives milk.
   It's a _______________.
2. This animal is grey. It is very big and very heavy.
   It's an _______________.
3. This animal has wings.
   It's a _______________.
4. This animal is brown. It has a long tail and a mane.
   It's a _______________.
5. This animal is pink. It likes mud.
   It's a _______________.
6. This animal is very small.
   It has eight legs.
   It's a _______________.

to give – geben
wings – die Flügel
tail – der Schwanz
mane – die Mähne
mud – der Schlamm

Lösung

dogs, elephants, sheep, lions, tigers, cows, bears, pigs, birds, spiders

1. cow
2. elephant
3. bird
4. lion
5. pig
6. spider

Where do they live?

Auf dieser Seite stehen viele Tiernamen. Entscheide, wo diese Tiere üblicherweise leben: **on a farm**, auf dem Bauernhof, **in the wild**, in der Wildnis oder **in the water**, im Wasser.

Male die Kästchen jeweils in der richtigen Farbe an.

On a farm **In the wild** **In the water**

lion
dog
cat
sheep
horse
elephant
koala
bear
fish
cow
pig
goat
hen
donkey
pony
frog
kangaroo
tiger
dolphin
crocodile

Lösung

On a farm: dog, cat, sheep, horse, pig, cow, goat, donkey, hen, pony

In the wild: elephant, lion, bear, koala, tiger, kangaroo

In the water: fish, dolphin, frog, crocodile

At the market

Lucy ist mit ihrem Papa auf dem Markt und kauft **fruit and vegetables**, Obst und Gemüse, ein. Vervollständige das Gespräch zwischen Lucy und dem Obsthändler. Wähle die passenden Sätze aus.

Lucy: ______________________________

Obsthändler: Hello! Can I help you?

Lucy: ______________________________

Obsthändler: Here you are. Ten apples.

Lucy: ______________________________

Obsthändler: Here you are. Five bananas.

Lucy: ______________________________

Obsthändler: It's one pound seventy.

Lucy: ______________________________

Obsthändler: Thank you. Bye!

1. And five bananas, please.
2. Hello!
3. Here you are. One pound seventy.
4. I'd like ten apples, please.
5. Thank you! How much does it cost?

Lösung

2, 4, 1, 5, 3

My school

Trage ein.

1. My school is: ____________________

2. My teacher's name is: ____________________

3. My class is: ____________________

4. I go to school at: ____________________ 

5. I come home at: ____________________ 

6. My favourite subjects are: ____________________

7. I sit next to: ____________________

8. I go school:

- [ ] on foot
- [ ] by bike
- [ ] by bus
- [ ] by car
- [ ] by tram

Lösung

Hier schreibst du deinen persönlichen **Schulsteckbrief**. Zeige ihn doch mal deinem Englischlehrer.

Find the school words

In dem Raster sind die englischen Übersetzungen von den folgenden zehn Wörtern, die mit Schule zu tun haben, versteckt. Findest du sie alle? Die Wörter sind vorwärts zu lesen – entweder waagerecht →, senkrecht ↓ oder diagonal ↘.

Stift Lehrer Kleber Bleistift Tafel

Klasse Schule Fach Schulbuch Schere

S	A	S	C	H	O	O	L	B	O	O	K
P	C	L	H	L	Z	R	U	I	Y	Q	B
R	I	H	E	R	A	F	B	N	A	S	A
P	K	C	O	G	C	S	J	G	L	U	E
E	W	P	Q	O	A	V	S	L	T	B	I
N	X	E	S	K	L	R	B	T	A	J	O
C	U	N	V	X	B	Q	S	E	L	E	R
I	V	G	A	B	W	T	Y	A	R	C	Z
L	L	H	W	E	X	U	K	C	I	T	G
S	C	I	S	S	O	R	S	H	F	H	A
F	G	H	T	Z	U	I	B	E	K	L	J
B	L	A	C	K	B	O	A	R	D	Y	O

Lösung

S	A	S	C	H	O	O	L	B	O	O	K
P	C	L	H	L	Z	R	U	I	Y	Q	B
R	I	H	E	R	A	F	B	N	A	S	A
P	K	C	O	G	C	S	J	G	L	U	E
E	W	P	Q	O	A	V	S	L	T	B	I
N	X	E	S	K	L	R	B	T	A	J	O
C	U	N	V	X	B	Q	S	E	L	E	R
I	V	G	A	B	W	T	Y	A	R	C	Z
L	L	H	W	E	X	U	K	C	I	T	G
S	C	I	S	S	O	R	S	H	F	H	A
F	G	H	T	Z	U	I	B	E	K	L	J
B	L	A	C	K	B	O	A	R	D	Y	O

Counting fish

Ui, im Meer wimmelt es ja nur so von Fischen! Wie viele Fische entdeckt Fips beim Tauchen? Zähle sie auf Englisch!

◯ red fish ◯ green fish ◯ yellow fish

◯ pink fish ◯ blue fish

Außerdem schwimmt im Meer:

◯ brown dog

Lösung

five red fish

one green fish

eight yellow fish

twelve pink fish

three blue fish

one brown dog

Around the year

a. Kreuze die Jahreszeiten an, die du auf Englisch schon benennen kannst.

b. Zu welcher Jahreszeit gehören diese Dinge? Verbinde die Bilder jeweils mit der richtigen Jahreszeit.

Lösung

The months

In diesem Kreis stehen die Monatsnamen. Trenne die Monatsnamen jeweils mit einem Strich. Zieh den Strich von der Mitte bis zum Rand und teile so den Kreis in 12 Stücke auf, wie bei einem Kuchen! Male anschließend deinen Jahreskuchen an – jeden Monat in einer passenden Farbe.

The seasons

Zu welcher Jahreszeit gehören die Monate? Male die Kästchen jeweils in der richtigen Farbe an.

spring summer autumn winter

August December January November June May April October February July March September

Lösung

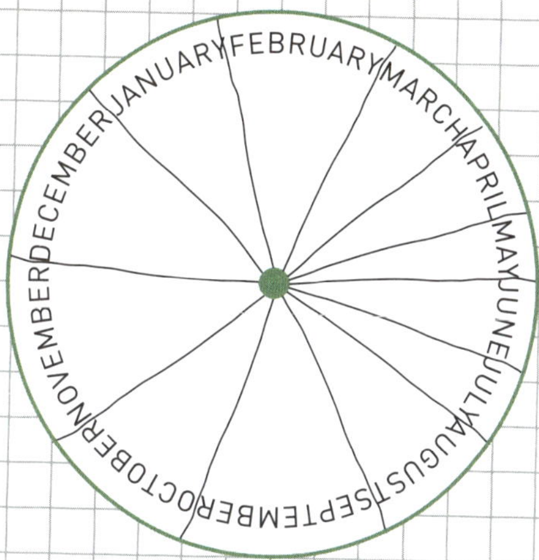

spring:	March, April, May
summer:	June, July, August
autumn:	September, October, November
winter:	December, January, February

My day

Jetzt bist du dran! Wie sieht dein Tag aus? Trage die Uhrzeiten ein und vervollständige die Sätze.

I get up at ______________________________

I go to school at ______________________________

I have lunch at ______________________________

I do my homework at ______________________________

I play with my friends at ______________________________

I go to bed at ______________________________

Viertel vor …, Viertel nach … und halb … drückst du auf Englisch so aus:

quarter to three – Viertel vor drei
quarter past three – Viertel nach drei
half past three – halb vier

Aufgepasst! Im Englischen bezieht sich **half past** auf die Stunde, die seit 30 Minuten vorbei ist!

Lösung

Magst du auch noch einen Tagesplan auf Englisch für Samstag oder Sonntag machen?

Numbers

Male die Kästchen jeweils in der richtigen Farbe an.

forty-five

ninety-three

18

61

sixty-one

20

79

fifty-seven

thirty-two

seventy-nine

32

45

84

eighty-four

twenty

sixty-six

93

66

eighteen

57

Lösung

How much does it cost?

Sicher weißt du schon, dass man in England nicht mit Euro zahlt, sondern mit **pounds** (Pfund) und **pence** (Pence). So sehen die Münzen in England aus:

1p 2p 5p 10p 20p 50p £1

So wie es das Zeichen **€** für Euro gibt, verwendet man in England **£** für Pfund und **p** für Pence. Wenn etwas ein Pfund und zehn Pence kostet, dann schreibt man es **£1.10**. Kostet etwas 50 Pence, schreibt man es **50p**.

Verbinde die Münzen jeweils mit dem richtigen Preisschild.

1. 

2. 

3. 

4. 

5. 

Lösung

1 = bread

2 = milk

3 = muffin

4 = hamburger

5 = apples